SAN FRANCISCO
Giants

JAMES R. ROTHAUS

CREATIVE EDUCATION

Published by Creative Education, Inc.
123 South Broad Street
Mankato, Minnesota 56001
Printed in the United States of America.

 ISBN 0-88682-150-9.

Cataloging in process information is available upon request from the publisher.

★ ★ ★

CONTENTS

COVER PHOTO
Mike Krukow won the Giants' Willie Mac team inspirational award for the second consecutive year. (1986)

PHOTO SPREAD (PAGE 2/3)
Rookie Power! Fresh from the minors, Will Clark went 6 for 9 at the plate in his role as Giants' pinch-hitter in key games. (1986)

San Francisco, Calif., is a city which sports the Golden Gate Bridge, cable cars, Fisherman's Wharf and one of the world's most fabled ball teams — the Giants.

Since 1958, loyal San Francisco Bay Area fans have braved dense fog and chilly ocean breezes to watch their Giants. Usually, by the time everyone settles into the seats at Candlestick Park, the bright sun burns through the mist. The spectators shed their jackets and soak up the warm California sun while shouting encouragement to their team.

They've cheered for San Francisco stars such as Willie Mays, Juan Marichal, Willie McCovey, Gary Matthews, Orlando Cepeda, Vida Blue, Johnny LeMaster and John Montefusco. These are only a handful of the great players who have proudly worn the Giants uniform. The all-time Giants roster reads like a roll call for the Hall of Fame. The Giants have been fielding feisty teams since 1876.

This is their story.

1876
The original club is founded in New York City.

Baseball After The Civil War

In 1883, a cigar-box manufacturer named John Day bought a baseball franchise. On May 1 of that year his New York team hosted a squad from Boston. General Ulysses S. Grant was in the stands, while two of the best pioneer ball players — William 'Buck' Ewing and John Montgomery Ward — were on the field for the "New Yorks," the club that would eventually become the Giants as the years wore on.

New York won that home opener. Slowly the team developed into strong contenders. With players like Ewing, New York couldn't miss.

PHOTO
Old "Long Pants" makes his 1939 debut. Here's Carl Hubbell, star Giants left-hander, breezing one through against the Cubs.

1883
John Day purchases the club. The following year, the team is christened the New York "Giants."

An all-around player whose face "seemed always on the verge of laughter," Ewing was called the best hitting and fielding catcher of the era. He was the only player in the nineteenth century to earn over $5,000 a year. He could bat lead-off or clean-up, and he was the first catcher to perfect the throw from a crouch.

In 1884, manager Jim Mutrie was so pleased by his team's powerful hitting and strong fielding that he shouted excitedly from the dugout: "My big fellows! My giants!" The New Yorks finally had a name.

Unfortunately, the Giants' success didn't continue during the 1890's. Mutrie retired in 1891, and the Giants went through 13 managers before a feisty little Irishman named John McGraw finally took the helm in 1902.

The John McGraw Era

McGraw was only 28, but he was determined to revive the Giants and make baseball a more respected profession. He did. Soon, everyone wanted to play for McGraw, despite his hot temper and harsh manner. His players traveled in style. They rode in the best trains, stayed in the finest hotels and were the highest-paid in the league.

McGraw could have lured any player he wanted into a Giants uniform, but he already had the best two pitchers in baseball at that time—maybe even of all time. Christy Mathewson and Iron Joe McGinnity were almost unbeatable on the mound.

PHOTO
The Irish legend. Feisty John McGraw skippered the New York Giants from 1902 to 1932, including four World Series in a row in the early 20's.

Joe McGinnity was an underhanded pitcher with a sharply breaking curveball. His arm was seemingly made of iron. Three times in August, 1903, he hurled

complete doubleheaders, winning all six games. Iron Joe had become a Giant a few years earlier when a scout told manager McCoskey about a young pitcher who had struck out 22 girls. McCoskey had a weak group of pitchers at the time. "Sign him up," he laughed. "You think one of my guys could strike out 22 girls?"

McGinnity went on to a 35-8 record in 1904.

McGraw had visions of a Giant dynasty. He knew he had a fine pitcher in McGinnity, and he saw the same qualities in Mathewson.

From the beginning, Matty was his pet project. Horace Fogel, the Giants manager before McGraw, had Christy pegged as a first baseman. After all, Fogel reasoned, he's big, strong and a steady fielder. Then McGraw arrived and said, "That's the dumbest thing I ever heard of. Mathewson has the most natural pitching motion I've ever seen."

He was right. Soon, the manager and star pitcher became fast friends. The Mathewsons even lived with the McGraws — the manager paid the heat bills and the rent while the hurler bought the groceries.

As a pitcher, Christy was such an immediate winner that a New York sportswriter quickly tagged him "Big Six," which meant the same as "the best." He was named after New York City's swiftest, most reliable fire engine company. The shy Mathewson, a handsome man with unruly blonde hair and clear, battleship-gray eyes, modestly said his nickname simply sprung from his being a six-footer.

But he definitely was "Old Reliable." Between 1903 and 1905, he won at least 30 games a season. If his legendary fadeaway pitch was off, his breaking curve took over.

1905
Giants pitcher Christy Mathewson pitches 27 scoreless innings in the World Series to lead the club to the World Championship.

PHOTO
Old Reliable.
This early batter was better-known for his awesome pitching. Christy Mathewson won more games in his career than any other pitcher in history, past or present.

1906
Legendary manager John McGraw is so sure his Giants will win the World Series, he has the team delivered to the stadium in carriages pulled by high-stepping horses. The words "World Champions" are sewn onto the bright yellow blankets covering the horses, but the team finishes second that year.

In 1904, the Giants won the pennant, but a disagreement among the leagues cancelled the World Series. The 1905 World Series was all Matty's. Within six days, he shut out the Phillies three times to lead New York to its first modern-day baseball title. He pitched 27 scoreless innings, struck out 18 and walked only one batter.

In 1908, he started 56 games — more than one-third of the season — and racked up a 37-11 record. He was billed by the press as a perfect man, "a Greek god in flannels." Christy didn't smoke, drink or gamble — he didn't like cards and wouldn't pitch on Sundays. He'd rather challenge nine people at once to a game of checkers or chess while wearing a blindfold!

The Giants visited the Series in 1911 but lost to Philadelphia, four games to two. They lost to the Yankees in 1912 in the same grand contest despite the early season tear of another Giant fireballer, Rube Marquard, who won his first 19 games.

Matty had another super year in 1913. Between June 19 and July 18, he hurled 68 consecutive innings — almost eight complete games — without granting a base on balls. During the entire season, he walked only 21 of the 1,195 men he faced!

Again Mathewson sparked the Giants into the Series. He won Game No. 2 for his fifth career Series victory. During that fall classic he worked 19 innings, allowed only three runs and had a 1.32 ERA.

Matty was traded to the Reds in 1916 and he turned Cincinnati into contenders. As a player, Mathewson had 373 career wins. Between 1903 and 1915 he won at least 20 games and on four occasions won over 30. Christy won more games than any other pitcher ever — more than Bob Grove and Dizzy Dean combined, more than Dazzy Vance and Carl Hubbel together. He still leads all National League pitchers with over 2,500 strike-outs. A member of the Hall of Fame, Mathewson's plaque simply states: "Matty was master of them all."

Despite the heroics of Mathewson and several other Giants, McGraw knew as early as 1913 that he needed to rebuild the core of his unit with younger players. He got to work right away.

1913
Mathewson pitches the "perfect month." From June 19 to July 18, he pitches 68 consecutive innings without giving up a single walk.

The Dynasty Of The Early 1920's

By 1921, McGraw's machine was terrorizing the National League. That year the Giants made their first of four straight trips to the World Series.

Frankie Frisch was a Giants hero in each Series. Always a steady performer, Frisch sparkled in October. He was the first man to bat at least .300 in four straight Series. In 1921 at age 22, he hit .300 against the Yanks and set a record for most putouts in a Series by a third baseman.

In the 1921 Series, the Giants didn't score a run until they were behind 4-0 in the third game. But Frisch's bat ignited his team to a come-from-behind 5-3 Series victory over the Yankees, the last of the best-of-nine championships.

The following year, the same teams met again and the Giants outslugged the Bronx Bombers once more. Even the Yankees' legendary Babe Ruth managed only 2 hits, batting a meek .118. As for McGraw's boys, Heinie Groh used his strange bottle-shaped bat to hit .474, followed by Frisch (.471), Ross Youngs (.375) and Frank Snyder (.333) for a combined team batting average of .309. Blistering hitting!

Some people say the 1923 World Series results should be recorded in the history books to read like this: New York Yankees, four games; the Giants' Casey Stengel, two games. The Giants failed to win their third straight World Championship, but Stengel's heroics kept the contest close. In one game he swatted a looping airball which cleared the fence for a game-winning homer. In another, he stretched a hit into an inside-the-park homer for the winning run.

In 1924, the Giants faced a new Series foe—the Washington Senators. The Series stretched to seven games. With the score tied in the twelfth inning, the tension was unbearable. Suddenly, the Senators' Earl McNeeley hit a routine hard-hopper to the steady Freddie Lindstrom at third. But the ball hit a pebble and bounced over Lindstrom's head. Washington used that break to score the winning run!

That final game marked the end of McGraw's winning era. In June, 1932, McGraw turned over the reins to Bill Terry, a man whom McGraw had coached and groomed carefully to take over his team.

McGraw had been with the Giants for 30 years. He had won 10 pennants, including four in a row, and he had directed the Giants to three World Championships.

1921
The Giants begin the "dynasty years" by making their first of four consecutive trips to the World Series under John McGraw.

Bill Terry Continues Winning Tradition

Terry proved to be as good a manager as he had been a player. As a hard-hitting Giant infielder, Terry had become the last National League hitter to bat over .400 when he achieved a .401 mark in 1930. His career average was .314—higher than Honus Wagner, Joe DiMaggio or Napoleon Lajoie. The 1930 MVP had also

PHOTO
Mel Ott, one of the smallest home-run threats to ever play the game, terrorized the league for the Giants until World War II.

June, 1932
John McGraw officially retires after guiding the Giants to 10 pennants and three world championships in his 30 years with the club.

led the league in assists and put-outs for five seasons.

In his first full season, Terry directed the club from the cellar to the 1932 pennant — the first of three in five years. Part of his success stemmed from employing himself in the field. He served as player/manager between 1932 and 1936. Following McGraw's example, he proved to be a wise field general. He, too, had an instinct for using the right player at the right time.

Of course, players like screwball artist Carl Hubbell made Terry's job much easier. Hubbell was always the right choice to send to the mound. Carl's nickname was "Meal Ticket." During those dreary days of the Depression, a meal ticket was like money in the bank — just as Hubbell was a sure thing to pitch a great game.

Like so many other great players, Hubbell had originally become a Giant because of John McGraw's ability to recognize great talent.

In 1928, McGraw had heard about a young screwball pitcher who was knocking everyone back to the dugout. Naturally, McGraw sent his best scout out to see this young ace.

"They say that screwball he pitches will ruin his arm," reported the scout, "and he won't be any good in another year or so."

"If that's all that's wrong with him," McGraw replied, "buy him. Matty had a screwball — they called it a fadeaway in those days — and he lasted pretty good."

As it turned out, McGraw's hunch about Hubbell was a great one. During one period which stretched between the 1936 and 1937 seasons, Hubbell won 24 consecutive games, completing 19 of them. He allowed only 159 hits in 207 innings, walking only 39 men. In 19 appearances he gave up three runs or less!

PHOTO
First baseman Bill Terry looked mighty fine at 1932 spring training. Later that year, he took over as manager and led the Giants to three pennant victories.

1932
In his first full season as manager, Bill Terry leads the Giants from the cellar to the N.L. Championship.

Hubbell's 1933 ERA was a low 1.66, and he hurled the Giants to two World Series victories, as New York embarrassed the Senators, four games to one.

The following year, the Dodgers barely edged the Giants for the flag. In 1935, New York fell to third place, but in 1938 they were winners once again.

Early in the season, the Giants were in fifth place, 11 games out of first. Then manager Terry took charge. On one July afternoon, he placed himself in the lineup despite his broken finger and sore legs. Boldly, he tore the splint from his finger and hobbled out to the diamond. He singled, doubled and tripled that day. After that, the Giants won 15 straight games, and 21 of the next 22. New York claimed the pennant and earned the right to meet the awesome Yanks in the World Championship battle.

Hubbell won the first game handily. In the second game, four Giant hurlers were shelled for 18 runs—every Yankee hit and scored. The Series was tied.

The turning point of the competition was Game Three—a real heartbreaker. Fred Fitzsimmons, the Giants' steady moundsman, held the Yanks to two hits. Unfortunately, one was a Lou Gehrig homer. In the eighth inning the score was knotted at one. The American League champs had a man on second and third when the batter hit a screamer back to Fitz. Fitz was the best fielding pitcher in the game, but this time he only got a piece of the ball. It glanced off his glove, a run scored. The Giants lost, 2-1. The Yankees went on to win the title in six games.

During Terry's reign, tiny Mel Ott developed into a Giant superstar. At 5-9, 170, Ott was probably the smallest home run threat ever to play the game. He came to the Giants in 1925—shy and scared and carrying a straw suitcase. He was only 16 when he stepped up to the plate (before the watchful eye of McGraw) to take some batting practice.

"Why do you raise your leg as you start to swing?" asked McGraw of Ott's funny habit of lifting his right foot during his cut.

"I always hit that way, Mr. McGraw. I guess it just comes natural to me."

"Then keep right on hitting that way. Don't let anybody change you," said McGraw, for he had noticed that the young man never moved his head or upper body during his swing. In fact, McGraw didn't want anyone fiddling with the boy's strange batting style. Under McGraw's direction, the kid from Louisiana never spent a day in the minors.

The year Ott turned 20 he hit .328 with 42 homers. During the 1933 World Series he nailed the Senators' Walter Steward for a two-run homer that one reporter said "would be a home run in any park in America—including Yellowstone."

Even though players like Hubbell and Ott continued to play strong baseball for the Giants, New York fell out of the pennant picture in 1937 and were never really a threat again until after World War II.

The 1950's Start With A Bang

The year 1951 was an awesome one for New York. The Giants were 13½ games behind the front-running Dodgers on August 11, but at the end of the regular season, the teams had identical records. A playoff for the pennant was necessary.

1934
Pitching in the All-Star Game, Carl Hubbell uses his screwball to retire five American League stars in a row, each of them future Hall-of-Famers—Babe Ruth, Lou Gehrig, Jimmy Fox, Al Simmons and Joe Cronin.

1951
Bobby Thomson launches a dramatic two-out, ninth-inning homer to give the Giants a come-from-behind victory over the Brooklyn Dodgers for the N.L. Championship. The Giants win the pennant!

The Giants won the first of the best-of-three series. Brooklyn forced a final game by winning the second.

In the third game, most people thought Brooklyn had sewed up the pennant. Going into the bottom of the ninth, the Dodgers led 4-1.

The first two Giants singled. Then Monte Irving (the hottest batter in the Series) popped out. Next, Whitey Lockman doubled in a run, and the score was 4-2 with men on second and third, one out. Bobby Thomson seemed nervous in the batter's box. He took the first pitch for a strike. When the next pitch came, he swung and connected.

"It's gonna be ... I believe ... the Giants win the pennant ... the Giants win the pennant ... the Giants win the pennant ... the Giants win the pennant ... Bobby hit it into the lower deck of the left-field stands ... the Giants win the pennant and they're going crazy ... I don't believe it ... I don't believe it ... I will not believe it ... Bobby Thomson hit a line-drive into the lower deck of the left-field stands and the place is going crazy ... and they're picking up Bobby Thomson and carrying him off the field ... the Giants win the pennant ..."

Those were the unforgettable words of Giants announcer Russ Hodges who would get so excited while broadcasting the games that he'd have to take tranquilizers to stop from yelling into the microphone.

Now Thomson was a hero. "Bobby toured the bases, leaping like an antelope. Before he had crossed the plate," wrote John Durant, a noted baseball historian, "ticker tape was streaming down from Wall Street windows, and Giants rooters the country over were dancing in the streets."

PHOTO
Here's Bobby Thomson hitting his famous home run in the Polo Grounds against the Brooklyn Dodgers in the 1951 playoff game.

1951
Willie Mays joins the Giants and runs off with Rookie of the Year honors.

Again the Giants were to face the Yankees, their cross-town rivals, in the World Series. The Yanks, who had won three of the last four championships, had defeated the Giants in the Series of 1923, 1936 and 1937. The Giants had a score to settle, and they set out to do so with a vengeance.

The Giants won the opener, 5-1. It was the first time since 1936 that the Yanks had lost the first game of a Series.

Monte Irvin sparked the Giants in the first three games to give his team the Series edge, 2-1. In the first game he had three singles and a triple. In the second he got three more singles and a double. During the entire Series, he had 11 hits in 24 at-bats for a .458 average. But his efforts weren't enough to carry the Giants. The Yankees took their 14th Crown in a six-game series.

Willie Mays Comes To Town

Although the Giants were disappointed in the World Series, 1951 had brought them one grand prize. A young outfielder named Willie Mays was brought up from the Minneapolis farm club after hitting a scorching .477. The young star was so loved in Minnesota that Giants owner Horace Stoneham had to place ads in the newspapers, apologizing and explaining why he needed Willie in New York City.

"He showed up at the Polo Grounds with six bats, a shaving kit and a toothbrush and . . . the biggest grin in Manhattan," recalled Hodges. "I'll never forget his pregame workout. Of course he was facing batting-practice pitching, but he belted it all over the place. He whistled line drives to all fields and smashed screaming wallops

PHOTO
Manager Leo Durocher had a lot to smile about as the Giants stormed into the decade of the 50's.

NY
NEW YORK

1954
Willie Mays leads the Giants to a four-game sweep over the Cleveland Indians in the World Series—the first Series sweep by a N.L. team in 40 years.

into the upper deck of the left-and centerfield stands. Then he went to the outfield where he cut loose with that marvelous arm, winging the ball from deep in center to third base and to the plate without a hop."

After watching Mays' pre-game heroics, Stoneham hollered to Manager Leo Durocher: "Hey, Leo! How do you like him?"

"I'll marry him," grinned Leo.

Somehow, Mays got off to a slow start during his first few days in the majors. He got very depressed and even told Durocher maybe he'd better go back to Minneapolis. But Leo said, "Don't worry, Willie. If you go 0 for 50, you're still my centerfielder. You're the greatest and don't forget it."

Indeed he was the greatest.

The "Say Hey Kid" came out of his brief slump and became the 1951 Rookie of the Year. He served in the Army in 1952 and 1953, but he returned in 1954 to run up 41 homers, 110 RBIs and a .354 batting average, a performance which earned him the MVP award. At 23, he was the youngest to ever receive that honor up to that time.

Willie led the Giants in the 1954 World Series against the Cleveland Indians — the American League champs who had won an amazing 111 games.

It was during this Series that Mays made one of the most memorable catches in baseball history. With the score tied, Mays made a spectacular over-the-shoulder catch of a Vic Wertz blast, grabbing the ball just before the warning track. Willie saved a sure run with that nab.

In the last of the ninth, the Giants' Dusty Rhodes sent a Bob Lemon pitch out of the park for a three-run homer. A pinch hitter, Rhodes was the Series hero. He had two hits and two homers in six at bats to drive in seven runs. He led the Series sweep for the Giants who became the 1954 World Champs. They were the first National League team to sweep the Series since the 1914 Braves.

1958
The Giants play their first season in San Francisco.

How The Giants Moved To San Francisco

The Giants fell into third place the next year and finished in sixth position in 1956 and 1957. During these disappointing years, many of the old Giants fans stopped coming to the Polo Grounds. Rumors began to spread that New York just wasn't big enough for three teams (Giants, Dodgers, Yanks).

First the Dodgers decided to move out West. The Giants followed their lead, so the famous Giants-Dodgers cross-town feud could continue as a California rivalry.

Beginning in 1958 the Giants of New York would become the Giants of San Francisco. It was a town that loved baseball and dearly wanted a major league team of its own.

New Yorkers screamed and demanded the team stay. They made speeches, wrote to newspaper editors and called their congressmen. They demanded in the names of old Giants greats like McGraw, Mathewson, Stengel, Ott and Hubble that the team stay put. But they still didn't come to the stadium in large enough numbers to root for the team.

In the next-to-last game of the season only 2,768 fans watched the Giants/Pirates game. But at the season finale, nearly 12,000 came to say good-bye. Some tears flowed. Many of the old-timers who had proudly worn

PHOTO SPREAD NEXT PAGE
The great one! After 14 seasons with the Phillies, Steve Carlton is shown throwing his first inning as a San Francisco Giant.

GIANTS

SAN FRANCISCO
SAN FRANCISCO

the New York colors were there for a special farewell ceremony.

The game itself was a disaster — the Giants lost 9-1. The real action occurred after the game. With the final out, thousands of spectators tumbled onto the field to grab a souvenir of the Giants' colorful history. The crowd fought over pieces of the bases. They ripped up the canopies which hung over the bullpens. Telephones were yanked out. The rubber padding on the outfield walls was torn off. People filled bottles with genuine Polo Ground dirt. The crowd chanted, "Stay, team, stay!" during the entire destruction of the Giants' home of 46 years.

Meanwhile, the players were in the clubhouse quietly packing up their equipment for the move out West to the land of orange groves and sunshine.

During the winter before the Giants' debut in San Francisco, over $1-million was raised in ticket sales.

Manager Bill Rigney held a press conference in 1958 to officially introduce Willie Mays to the local reporters. Everyone in New York loved Mays, and Rigney wanted people of San Francisco to do the same.

"Willie Mays is the world's greatest athlete," he began. "His motions are so smooth I even get a kick out of the silky way he puts on his coat. He is the only man known who can win a game for you in every department of the game, except pitching. They talk about his impossible catches. In 1957, we were leading Pittsburgh by a couple runs in the late innings and the Pirates loaded the bases. Roberto Clemente smashed one that should have been a triple. No other centerfielder in the N.L. could have gotten that ball, I'll swear, but we know Willie. We watched him start the chase to his

1962
Mays blasts 40 homers to lead the Giants to their first N.L. Pennant for the San Francisco fans.

PHOTO
In 1958 the Giants of New York became the Giants of San Francisco. Between celebrations, manager Bill Rigney took a moment to pose with the great Willie Mays.

1965
Willie Mays hits an all-time club high of 52 homers.

right. We waited for him to punch the glove—his instinctive signal that he's got it. We waited some more. It was a tremendous wallop and I groaned. But hold it! To this minute I don't know how, but Willie got there, except he didn't have time or room to put out his gloved hand. Know what he did? He reached up with his bare hand and clutched it for the out. After that stunner to retire the side, Willie trotted to the dugout where he placed the ball in my hand. He smiled just a little bit, from the corners, and he said, 'Here's something for you, Skipper.' "

Willie had a strong season that first year in California, but San Francisco's first hero was a rookie named Orlando Cepeda. He hit .312, was named Rookie of the Year and was voted Most Valuable Giant by a newspaper survey.

The Giants finished third in 1958, but Giants fever was spreading all over Northern California. One survey said that over 70 percent of all the radios in the Bay Area were tuned to the 1959 opener.

In 1959, the Giants farm system produced another Rookie of the Year award-winner. Willie McCovey had two triples and two singles in his first game for the Giants. San Francisco won six of the first seven games he played in. He collected five singles, two doubles, three triples and three homers. Even though he played only half the season, he won the best rookie award easily.

PHOTO
The legendary Willie Mays looks down the third base line for the "hit away" signal in 1968 game action.

San Francisco Gets Its First Pennant

With stars like Mays, Cepeda and McCovey, San Franciscans were optimistic about their team being

1968
Juan Marichal pitches for 26 victories, a club record that still stands.

a real contender. In 1962, they got their wish.

The Giants had a poor pre-season but on opening day, everything came together. Second-year pitcher Juan Marichal shut out the Braves' Warren Spahn, 6-0. Mays connected for his first of 40 regular-season four-baggers. The Giants were off.

In past years, the Giants had a tendency to fall out of the pennant race early. But not this year.

San Francisco was four games behind the Dodgers with 13 games to go, but manager Alvin Dark, in his second year at the Giants helm, wasn't worried. "The race will go down to the last day. We aren't through."

He was right.

The Giants won seven in a row, and they caught Los Angeles because the Dodgers fell apart.

"The Dodgers died at their own hands," explained sportswriter Art Rosenbaum. "Tired of looking back at the tenacious Giants who seemed almost carefree, and a little frightening, too, the Dodgers stopped hitting, kept losing and were caught on closing day."

The California foes were headed to a three-game playoff. Dark again predicted the future. "We'll win it now, and we'll take the Yankees to seven games in the World Series."

The special play-off was almost a repeat of the exciting '51 New York/Brooklyn squeaker which the Giants had won on Bobby Thomson's ninth-inning homer.

Giants top of the ninth. The scoreboard showed the Dodgers leading, 4-2. A single, a force, a walk, a walk, and the bases were loaded. Willie Mays was up. Willie slapped a hard slider back to pitcher Ed Roebuck who deflected it. A run scored. Bases still loaded.

Orlando Cepeda was in the box, and he had been in a

slump. The Giants fans groaned. They remembered how Cepeda had popped out in the first, hit into a double play with bases loaded in the third and left a run stranded in the seventh by hitting into a force.

Stan Williams replaced Roebuck on the mound, but Cepeda hammered a sacrifice fly deep into right to drive in a run. The score was tied.

The bases were loaded again after a wild pitch and a walk. Shortstop Jose Pagan nailed another Dodger hurler for a hard grounder which Larry Burright kicked for an error.

"The Dodgers, leading 4-2, had been pressed into four walks, one wild pitch, two deflections, one that was scored an official error and both could have been outs, and four big runs," reported Rosenbaum.

The Giants retired the Dodgers easily in the last of the ninth and were crowned the National League champs. They headed home to Candlestick to meet their age-old rivals, the New York Yankees.

Just as Dark had predicted, the Series stretched to seven games.

San Francisco had the statistical edge in most categories—better pitching, more hits, more runs, more doubles, more triples, more homers. Still, in the bottom of the ninth, the Giants were one out away from losing to the Yanks again.

Now, Series hero Willie McCovey was up. Throughout the championship, McCovey had shown what a complete player he truly was. He started the second and fifth games at first base, the third in right field and the final game in left. He hadn't made any errors; he had smashed a homer in the second game to lead the Giants to a 2-0 victory.

1969
The great Willie McCovey hits 45 homers—an all-time Giant record for a southpaw.

1972
After 22 years with the Giants, living legend Willie Mays is traded to the New York Mets.

The entire city of San Francisco and each of his teammates knew McCovey could win the game for the Giants. He took a mighty swing at the next pitch and the ball sailed away—right to a waiting outfielder.

If McCovey had hit the ball just an inch more toward right, it surely would have been a homer. "No human can hit a ball harder. Nor with lousier luck," sighed a disheartened sportswriter.

But the crowd of nearly 44,000 was very proud of its team. The Giants had given San Francisco its first pennant in a thrilling, unforgettable season. San Francisco was a city of champions.

Giants In The Modern Era

Each year since their 1962 World Series appearance, the Giants have struggled valiantly to win another pennant. Only once since the divisional play-off system began in 1969 have they actually won the Western Conference title. In 1971, they lost to the Pirates in the National League playoffs, but they came right back in the years to follow, struggling to capture their old magic.

During those years several super players proudly wore the brilliant black and orange of the Giants.

Mike McCormick won the Cy Young Award in 1967. McCovey was the 1969 Most Valuable Player.

Willie Mays played brilliantly for the Giants for 22 years before he was finally traded to the New York Mets in 1972 so he could finish his career in the city where it began. At the end of the 1981 season, Mays still held 13 team records.

Bobby Bonds roamed the Giants outfield from 1968 to 1974, and set an all-time San Francisco record by

PHOTO
Shown breaking from the plate is switch-hitter Chili Davis. (1986)

SF

scoring 134 runs in a single season.

Hard-hitting outfielder Gary Matthews was named Rookie of the Year in 1973. Pitcher John "The Count" Montefusco won the award in 1975, winning 15 and striking out 215.

Johnny LeMaster came up through the Giants' productive minor-league system to become their starting shortstop a few years later. LeMaster became the 43rd player in the majors to hit a homer in his first big-league at bat when he nailed the Dodgers' Don Sutton for an inside-the-park home run in 1975.

The list of individual honors and achievements goes on and on, growing deeper and more impressive with each new season. As a team, however, the Giants of the modern era have struggled, to say the least. To be a Giants fan in the 1980's has usually been a lesson in frustration. Seldom has a big-league baseball club shown so much promise for so many years with so little to show for it. Check it out:

The 1980 season was supposed to be a "great one" for San Francisco, and it really was . . . "except for the beginning and the end," mused Manager Dave Bristol who was fired at the conclusion of a disappointing 75-86 campaign.

Replacing Bristol in 1981 was rookie manager Frank Robinson — yeah, that's the guy — the same Frank Robinson who had starred as the outfield flash of the Reds and Orioles. Robinson, the National League's first black skipper, was now determined to lead the Giants back into the pennant races.

Though his club started slowly in '81, Robinson took advantage of a mid-season players' strike to re-think his strategy and shuffle some key positions in the lineup. It

1973
Gary Matthews captures Rookie of the Year honors.

PHOTO
Another Giants big-stick. Outfielder Gary Matthews took Rookie of the Year honors in 1973.

1975
John "The Count" Montefusco strikes out 215 batters on his way to winning Rookie of the Year honors.

PHOTO
First Baseman Orlando Cepeda is one second away from picking off Pirate Gino Cimoli in 1960 double-header.

worked. When the strike ended, Robinson's new-look Giants tore up the league. They remained in playoff contention until the final week, finishing 56-55—their first winning season since 1973!

The following year—1982—Robinson showed up at spring training, took one good look at his players and brashly predicted, "The Giants could go all the way this season!"

Inspired by the vote of confidence, Robinson's players rallied together for an outstanding 87-75 season, finishing in third-place just two games behind Atlanta. Two wily old veterans—Joe Morgan, 39, and Reggie Smith, 37—provided leadership and batting power. But it was the Giants' bullpen, sparked by Greg Minton and Al Holland, that saved the day so many times throughout the '82 season.

"The Giants exhibited character," wrote Nick Peters in the *Official Baseball Guide*, "rallying for 45 of their victories, including 27 on their final at-bats. They topped the majors in one-run games (66) and one-run victories (38).

"By going 21-8 down the stretch, the Giants posted consecutive winning seasons for the first time since 1970-71. The spree included their first three-game sweep at Dodger Stadium in 15 years, and there was a measure of satisfaction in knocking the Dodgers out of a pennant playoff against Atlanta with a 5-3 victory (thanks to a dramatic Joe Morgan homer) on the final day of the season."

Then came 1983. Buoyed by the strong finish of a year before, Robinson again went out on a limb and predicted a championship season for his Giants. Oh, how the San Francisco fans hoped he was right. Oh,

how their hopes came tumbling down as the season wore on.

"Our biggest problem was inconsistency," said Robinson about the team's fifth-place finish. "I never knew which team would show up at the ball park. One day we were unbeatable, and the next we were pushovers. It was frustrating."

Not as frustrating as the next two seasons would be.

1981
Frank Robinson takes over as Giants manager, becoming the first black skipper in N.L. history.

The Giants Sag, And Robinson Says Good-Bye

Back in 1982, the Giants had celebrated their 25th anniversary in San Francisco. In honor of the many great players who had served the city, a "San Francisco Dream Team" had been selected by the fans. The stars named to the team were: Tom Haller, catcher; Willie McCovey, first; Tito Fuentes, second; Jim Davenport, third; Johnnie LeMaster, shortstop; Gary Matthews, left field; Willie Mays, center; Jack Clark, right; Orlando Cepeda, infield/outfield; Juan Marichal, right-handed pitcher; Vida Blue, left-handed pitcher; Stu Miller, right-handed relief pitcher; Al Holland, left-handed relief pitcher. And, last but not least, a proud and deeply-touched Frank Robinson had been named as the manager of the San Francisco Dream Team.

Now, just two years later, on August 4, 1984, Robinson was dismissed as manager, forced to leave his beloved Giants with a dismal record of 42-64 for the season, and getting worse. A sad series of injuries had beset the club (nine starters had gone on the disabled list at times during the season), and . . . well, Robinson had done his best to make adjustments, but it was obvious that the players had lost confidence in themselves.

PHOTO
Manager Frank Robinson—the former outfield great—led the Giants into the 1980's with a dream, a plan and a smile.

1982
The Giants celebrate their 25th anniversary in San Francisco, and the fans select the "San Francisco Dream Team."

Meanwhile, the disappointed Giants fans were steadily losing interest in the team. Attendance for 1984 plummeted to one million, the lowest mark in many years. Owner Bob Lurie threatened to sell the franchise at the end of the season, and the players' morale hit rock-bottom.

Maybe that's why the 1985 Giants lost 100 games for the first time in franchise history. Nothing went right that year. Nothing. "We started off on a sour note, and that sort of set the tone for the whole season," said southpaw pitcher Dave LaPoint. "Within a few weeks, we were already at the point where we were just putting on the uniform and playing out the schedule."

Could the Giants bounce back from such a dismal season? "You better believe it!" said rookie third baseman Chris Brown who lead the '85 Giants with a .271 average while hitting 16 homers and driving in 61. "Yes, we had a bad year. Sure, we're a little down right now, but the important thing is, we're not down on each other. No sweat — we'll be back in '86, then watch out."

The Turnaround Season Of '86

When the Giants took to the field for the beginning of the 1986 season, they appeared to be the same guys who had flopped the year before. Same uniforms. Same stadium. Same owner. The only big difference was a new manager by the name of Roger Craig, but he was all that was necessary to revive the ailing Giants and lead them to a winning season!

Craig had been around for the last 18 games of the previous season, and he had come away with two observations:

PHOTO
Slugger Chris Brown led the Giants with a sparkling .317 batting average in 1986.

BROWN
35

BONDS
25

First, the Giants had lots of talent, but no discipline.

Second, the Giants had lots of good hitters, but none of them were hitting the ball.

During spring training, therefore, Craig led the team through hour after hour of the most fundamental hitting and fielding drills. "We're getting back to basics," he explained. "If we can discipline ourselves to do the little things right, then the big things will take care of themselves."

The San Francisco fans must have liked what they heard because they returned to Candlestick Park by the thousands in 1986. Attendance increased by more than 500,000 over '85. Inspired, the Giants responded with a turnaround season in all departments, but especially in the hitting.

"Our bats came alive again," beamed Al Rosen, the Giants' popular new General Manager at season's end. "Our bench was magnificent in the pinch," he punned. Rosen's stat sheet told an amazing tale:

• San Francisco pinch-hitters led the majors with 10 home runs and 59 RBIs.

• Candy Maldonado broke Duane Kuiper's club mark of 14 pinch-hits, and led all major league pinch-hitters in homers (four) and RBIs (20).

• Harry Spilman batted .406 as a pinch-hitter, including nine RBIs, three of them game-winners.

• Rick Lancellotti batted .308 in the pinch, including two homers and six runs batted in.

• Last but not least, rookie first baseman Will Clark went 6 for 9 (that's .667!) as a pinch-hitter.

Remember that fantastic 1982 season when the Giants pulled out 27 victories in their final at-bat? Well, this 1986 team showed that kind of gumption. In all,

1986
The Giants under Manager Roger Craig post a brilliant turnaround by pulling out 39 victories, 26 of them won in the final at-bat.

PHOTO
Somehow, Bobby Bonds would get on base and score. He set an all-time San Francisco record for most tallies in a single season—134!

1987
Heading into the first part of the season, the Giants under Roger Craig are picked by Sports Illustrated as the "team most likely to surprise the rest of the league."

they posted 39 come-from-behind victories, 26 of them won in their final at-bat!

"I'm so proud of these guys," said pitcher Mike Krukow who won the Willie Mac Award as the Giants' most inspirational player for the second straight year. "I'm proud of the fans, too, because so many have hung in there with us even though we've had some terribly disappointing times over the past few years."

After the brilliant turnaround in 1986, the Giants decided to renew manager Roger Craig's contract for 1987 and 1988. The City of San Francisco rejoiced. As for Craig, he was too busy to celebrate.

"We've got work to do," said the hard-charging manager in his typical soft-serious voice. "It's nice to win some games, but the Giants won't rest until we win the big one."

Stay tuned. It's simply a matter of time before another pennant waves from the pole above the bleachers in Candlestick Park!

PHOTO
Great in a pinch! Candy Maldonado broke the club record of 14 pinch-hits, and led all major league pinch-hitters in homers (4) and RBIs (20) in the 1986 campaign.